Little Hymns®

Little Hymns • Fairest Lord Jesus
Written and illustrated by Andy Holmes
Watercolor by Cameron Thorp
Music transcription by Marty Franks

First Printing 1993
ISBN 0-929216-58-X
Printed in the United States of America

Published by

PRESS

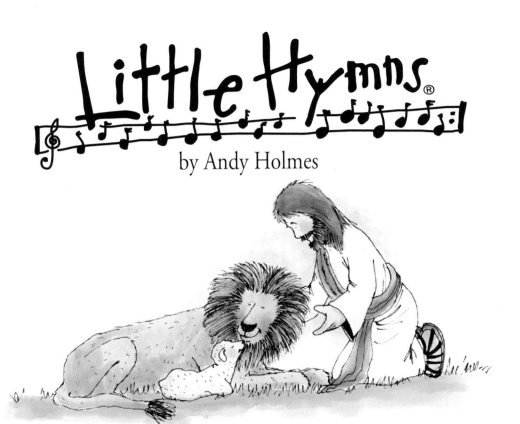

Fairest Lord Jesus

Fair - est Lord Je - sus,

Rul - er of all na - ture,

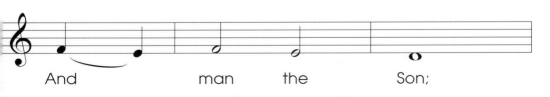

And   man   the   Son;

Thee   will   I   cher   -   ish,

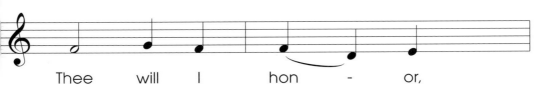

Thee will I hon - or,

Fair   are   the   mead - ows,

Fair - er still the wood - lands,

Robed in the bloom - ing garb of Spring;

Je - sus is fair - er,

Je - sus is pur - er,

Who makes the woe-ful heart to sing.

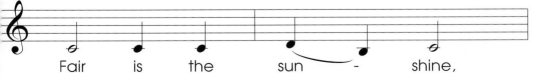

Fair   is   the   sun - shine,

And all the twin-kling, star - ry host;

Je - sus shines bright - er,

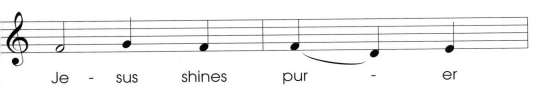

Je - sus shines pur - er

Than all the an - gels heaven can boast.

Fairest Lord Jesus